CHLOË LAWRENCE-TAYLOR

Chloë has been commissioned by NT Connections and the Royal Court Theatre's Living Archive, and is on attachment to the National Theatre.

Personal Values is her debut play.

Other Titles in this Series

Annie Baker
THE ANTIPODES
THE FLICK
INFINITE LIFE
JOHN

Mike Bartlett
THE 47TH
ALBION
BULL
GAME
AN INTERVENTION
KING CHARLES III
MIKE BARTLETT PLAYS: TWO
MRS DELGADO
SCANDALTOWN
SNOWFLAKE
UNICORN
VASSA *after* Gorky
WILD

Jack Bradfield
THE HABITS

Jessie Cave
SUNRISE

Mohamed-Zain Dada
BLUE MIST
DIZZY
SPEED

Beth Flintoff
THE BALLAD OF MARIA MARTEN
THE GLOVE THIEF
REBELLIOUS WOMEN

JJ Green
A-TYPICAL RAINBOW

Lucy Kirkwood
BEAUTY AND THE BEAST
 with Katie Mitchell
BLOODY WIMMIN
THE CHILDREN
CHIMERICA
HEDDA after Ibsen
THE HUMAN BODY
IT FELT EMPTY WHEN THE HEART
 WENT AT FIRST BUT IT IS
 ALRIGHT NOW
LUCY KIRKWOOD PLAYS: ONE
MOSQUITOES
NSFW
RAPTURE
TINDERBOX
THE WELKIN

Benedict Lombe
LAVA
SHIFTERS

Haley McGee
AGE IS A FEELING

Charley Miles
BLACKTHORN
DAUGHTERHOOD
THERE ARE NO BEGINNINGS

Chloë Moss
CHRISTMAS IS MILES AWAY
CORRINA, CORRINA
FATAL LIGHT
THE GATEKEEPER
HOW LOVE IS SPELT
RUN SISTER RUN
THIS WIDE NIGHT
THE WAY HOME

Lucy Roslyn
PENNYROYAL

Sam Steiner
KANYE THE FIRST
LEMONS LEMONS LEMONS LEMONS
 LEMONS
A TABLE TENNIS PLAY
YOU STUPID DARKNESS!

Jack Thorne
2ND MAY 1997
AFTER LIFE *after* Hirokazu Kore-eda
BUNNY
BURYING YOUR BROTHER IN
 THE PAVEMENT
A CHRISTMAS CAROL *after* Dickens
THE END OF HISTORY…
HOPE
JACK THORNE PLAYS: ONE
JACK THORNE PLAYS: TWO
JUNKYARD
LET THE RIGHT ONE IN
 after John Ajvide Lindqvist
THE MOTIVE AND THE CUE
MYDIDAE
THE SOLID LIFE OF SUGAR WATER
STACY & FANNY AND FAGGOT
WHEN WINSTON WENT TO WAR WITH
 THE WIRELESS
WHEN YOU CURE ME
WOYZECK *after* Büchner

debbie tucker green
BORN BAD
DEBBIE TUCKER GREEN PLAYS: ONE
DIRTY BUTTERFLY
EAR FOR EYE
HANG
NUT
A PROFOUNDLY AFFECTIONATE,
 PASSIONATE DEVOTION TO SOMEONE
 (– NOUN)
RANDOM
STONING MARY
TRADE & GENERATIONS
TRUTH AND RECONCILIATION

Tom Wells
BIG BIG SKY
BROKEN BISCUITS
DRIP *with* Matthew Robins
FOLK
JUMPERS FOR GOALPOSTS
THE KITCHEN SINK
ME, AS A PENGUIN

Chloë Lawrence-Taylor

PERSONAL VALUES

NICK HERN BOOKS
London
www.nickhernbooks.co.uk

A Nick Hern Book

Personal Values first published in Great Britain in 2025 as a paperback original by Nick Hern Books Limited, The Glasshouse, 49a Goldhawk Road, London W12 8QP

Personal Values copyright © 2025 Chloë Lawrence-Taylor

Chloë Lawrence-Taylor has asserted her moral right to be identified as the author of this work

Cover image: jaturonoofer via iStock

Designed and typeset by Nick Hern Books, London
Printed in the UK by Mimeo Ltd, Huntingdon, Cambridgeshire PE29 6XX

A CIP catalogue record for this book is available from the British Library

ISBN 978 1 83904 459 5

CAUTION All rights whatsoever in this play are strictly reserved. Requests to reproduce the text in whole or in part should be addressed to the publisher.

Amateur Performing Rights Applications for performance, including readings and excerpts, by amateurs in the English language throughout the world should be addressed to the Performing Rights Department, Nick Hern Books, The Glasshouse, 49a Goldhawk Road, London W12 8QP, *tel* +44 (0)20 8749 4953, *email* rights@nickhernbooks.co.uk, except as follows:

Australia: ORiGiN Theatrical, Level 1, 213 Clarence Street, Sydney NSW 2000, *tel* +61 (2) 8514 5201, *email* enquiries@originmusic.com.au, *web* www.origintheatrical.com.au

New Zealand: Play Bureau, 20 Rua Street, Mangapapa, Gisborne, 4010, *tel* +64 21 258 3998, *email* info@playbureau.com

United States and Canada: Casarotto Ramsay and Associates Ltd, see details below

Professional Performing Rights Applications for performance by professionals in any medium and in any language throughout the world (including by stock companies in the USA and Canada) should be addressed to Casarotto Ramsay and Associates Ltd, *email* rights@casarotto.co.uk, www.casarotto.co.uk

No performance of any kind may be given unless a licence has been obtained. Applications should be made before rehearsals begin. Publication of this play does not necessarily indicate its availability for amateur performance.

www.nickhernbooks.co.uk/environmental-policy

Nick Hern Books' authorised representative in the EU is
Easy Access System Europe – Mustamäe tee 50, 10621 Tallinn, Estonia
email gpsr.requests@easproject.com

For Mum and Dad

Personal Values was first performed at Hampstead Theatre Downstairs, London, on 11 April 2025, with the following cast:

VEDA	Holly Atkins
BEA	Rosie Cavaliero
ASH	Archie Christoph-Allen
Director	Lucy Morrison
Set Designer	Naomi Dawson
Associate Designer and Costume Designer	Hannah Schmidt
Lighting Designer	Holly Ellis
Sound Designer	Max Pappenheim
Production Manager	Josh Collins
Stage Manager	Oliwia Rokowska

Acknowledgements

I would like to thank the kind people who have lent their brilliant minds to the creation of this play:

Phillippe Cato, Helena Clark, Pip Cull, Jane Fallowfield, Daisy Hall, Alice Hamilton, Hector Rodríguez Manchego, Rachel Taylor, and all at Hampstead Theatre and Nick Hern Books.

Thank you, Lucy Morrison, for your rigour, hard graft, humour, and extraordinary care.

Thank you, Gee.

And always, thank you to my family and to my partner – your support has made this play possible.

C.L-T.

Characters

BEA
VEDA
ASH

Setting

Bea's two-up-two-down house.
Her home should not look like a house.
Her home should not look like it is made of bricks and mortar.
It should look like it is made of cookbooks and catalogues and radios and storage bags.

Staging

Resist naturalism.
Characters can stay on stage the entire time.
Costume changes can happen onstage.
There is no need to hide anything.

Notes on the Text

A dash (–) signals a sharp change in flow.
A slash (/) indicates where the next speech begins.
An ellipsis (…) occurs when one or more characters no longer know what to say.
Any words that have been ~~struck through~~ should be conveyed without being spoken.

This text went to press before the end of rehearsals and so may differ slightly from the play as performed.

ACT ONE

Scene One

BEA*'s densely packed, precariously balanced, over-stuffed lounge.*

BEA *wears yellow washing-up gloves.*

VEDA. It's alpaca.

BEA. What?

VEDA. It's pure wool.

BEA. Smells like wet dog.

VEDA. It'll warp if you use a flimsy hanger like that.

BEA. What will?

VEDA. The shape.

BEA. Oh.

VEDA. Best to let it dry flat.

BEA. Bit short on flat surfaces.

VEDA. Then I'll keep it on.

BEA. It's sopping.

VEDA. It's fine.

BEA. You're shivering.

VEDA. I'm fine.

BEA. I couldn't get to the door / any –

VEDA. / Don't lie.

BEA. I'm not lying.

VEDA. You are.

BEA. I'm not.

VEDA. Frosted glass doesn't hide everything, I saw you duck down.

BEA. I wasn't hiding.

VEDA. You were but I'm not going to argue the point.

BEA. I have no reason to hide.

VEDA. Good for you.

BEA. I'm actually a little bit in-the-middle of something.

VEDA. I don't really care.

BEA. That's nice of you.

VEDA. You painted the door.

BEA. It was peeling.

VEDA. It's… mustardy.

BEA. It's turmeric.

VEDA. It's a statement.

BEA. Water got under the paint.

VEDA. Bottom of our door is rotten, it's all the rain.

BEA. You should do something about that.

VEDA. I've been waiting for Sid to do something about it.

BEA. Better get used to it then.

VEDA. Strange how a man can spend so much time in his shed and produce almost nothing at all.

BEA. Your coat is dripping.

VEDA. You got my hopes up.

BEA. What?

VEDA. With the door.

BEA. And?

VEDA. Not much changes here.

BEA. The neighbours like it.

VEDA. Yeah?

BEA. It's gotten quite a lot of compliments.

VEDA. Didn't know you were so houseproud.

   BEA *is wounded*.

   It looks lovely.

BEA. What are you doing here?

VEDA. Just dropping by.

BEA. Be honest.

VEDA. Just paying you a little visit.

BEA. Why?

VEDA. Because it's a nice thing to do.

BEA. Bullshit.

VEDA. Such a warm welcome.

BEA. You should've called.

VEDA. And given you the chance to escape?

BEA. Yes.

VEDA. Better to ask for forgiveness than permission.

BEA. Are you taking your coat off or what?

VEDA. Not just yet.

BEA. Suit yourself.

VEDA. Have you been cooking… sausages?

BEA. No.

VEDA. Oh.

BEA. Why?

VEDA. Nothing.

BEA. Why?

VEDA. It's just…

BEA. You smell sausages?

VEDA. A bit.

BEA. I can't smell sausages.

VEDA. There's definitely something… sausagey.

>VEDA *sniffs*.
>
>BEA *sniffs too*.
>
>VEDA *follows her nose to the fan heater*.

Here's the culprit.

BEA. I still don't smell sausages.

VEDA. I quite like it actually.

>VEDA *places her hands on the fan heater*.

BEA. Careful!

VEDA. Nice and warm.

BEA. You'll burn yourself.

VEDA. At least I'd be warm.

BEA. Sit.

VEDA. Where?

BEA. There.

VEDA. That's your chair.

BEA. I can hear your teeth chattering.

VEDA. You're the one who kept me outside.

BEA. Take those boots off.

VEDA. Really?

BEA. Before you sit down – you're squelching.

VEDA. You're fussing.

BEA. They're saturated.

VEDA. They're not.

BEA. You'll get trench foot.

VEDA. I'm not going to get trench foot.

BEA. Take them off.

VEDA. Fine.

BEA. Then put them there on the mat.

VEDA. You love the whole ~~mothering~~ routine, don't you?

BEA. No, I just don't like mudandrainandshit all over my carpet.

VEDA. I've not got shit on your carpet.

BEA. Not literal shit.

VEDA (*pulling her boots off*). Happy?

BEA. Ecstatic.

VEDA. Phew.

BEA. I could've been out.

VEDA. I'd have waited.

BEA. I could've been out all day.

VEDA. I would've waited as long / as

BEA. / I could've been away.

VEDA. But you're not.

BEA. Not right now.

VEDA. Remind me when your last getaway was?

...

Either way we're both here now.

BEA. Your lucky day.

VEDA. It feels it.

BEA. So what's the bad news?

VEDA. Is there another chair somewhere?

BEA. Why?

VEDA. Because I'm going to sit and I don't want you hovering.

BEA. I don't feel like sitting.

VEDA. Such a hoverer.

BEA. I'm not a hoverer.

VEDA. Do you not have another chair?

BEA. Course I do.

VEDA. Where?

BEA. I don't need to show you.

VEDA. Do you really only have one chair left that's…?

   BEA *pulls out a folding camping chair.*

BEA. It's space-saving.

   VEDA *sits in* BEA*'s armchair.*

VEDA. That's Dad's.

   BEA *bristles.*

Vest and a moustache and you'd look just like him.

   BEA *frosts over.*

I'm allowed to talk about Dad.

BEA. Never said you weren't.

VEDA. I'm just saying.

BEA. Well just because you're 'just saying' doesn't mean I have to 'just say' anything back, okay?

VEDA. Okay.

BEA. What way did you come?

VEDA. What?

BEA. Motorway or the lanes?

VEDA. Really?

BEA. Really.

VEDA. If this is what we're doing: the lanes.

BEA. They've reopened?

VEDA.... Yes.

BEA. There was a horrendous accident the other day, just after the bit where you come out of the woods and it drops down to thirty miles per hour, they were kids, teenagers, one's head was... decapitated.

VEDA. You need to practise your small talk.

BEA. Is Ash alright?

VEDA. He's... Ash.

BEA. Is he driving?

VEDA. No.

BEA. Good.

VEDA. It's not good.

BEA. I think it's good.

VEDA. No, if he was driving he'd have somewhere to go but he doesn't need to learn because he doesn't have anywhere to go.

BEA. He's only little.

VEDA. He's not.

BEA. Still.

VEDA. The extent of his driving experience is *World of Tanks*.

BEA. What?

VEDA. A game.

BEA. Oh.

VEDA. He's not little any more, Bea.

BEA. No.

VEDA. He's taller than Sid.

BEA. Jesus.

VEDA. It's freaky.

BEA. How's Sid?

VEDA. Don't know, not asked.

BEA. Shed finished yet?

VEDA. He's living in it.

BEA. That's –

VEDA. Don't.

BEA. I'm not –

VEDA. We've got to get over ourselves.

BEA. What?

VEDA. We have got to get over ourselves, Bea.

BEA. You can go first.

VEDA. I don't think all that much of myself you know.

BEA. Don't you?

VEDA. A lot has changed.

BEA. Then what's with the coat?

VEDA. What?

BEA. 'It's pure wool… alpaca.'

VEDA. I've not let myself go completely.

BEA. Never knowingly underdressed.

ACT ONE, SCENE ONE 17

VEDA. I had to see you.

BEA. And now you have.

VEDA. I wanted to see you.

BEA. What I want never really comes into it.

VEDA. I had to see what your life looked like.

BEA. Nothing you haven't seen before.

VEDA. It's worse.

BEA. It's not.

VEDA. We have to stop accepting it.

BEA. You mean me.

VEDA. No.

BEA. None of this has anything to do with you.

VEDA. That's not true.

BEA. Stop.

VEDA. I have no interest in stopping.

BEA. Then can you just fuck off home?

VEDA. I've imagined it a lot.

BEA. Have you now?

VEDA. It makes me so sad.

BEA. Just imagining it?

VEDA. And, now, being here, it's all I feel.

BEA. You feel sad?

VEDA. Yes.

BEA. Well, don't let it get you down.

VEDA. Can't help it.

BEA. Try.

VEDA. I am.

BEA. Try harder.

VEDA. I have.

BEA. Not hard enough.

VEDA. Are you happy?

BEA. Are you?

VEDA. No.

> …
>
> No I'm not happy.
> I'm fuming.
> And I feel… lacking… in so much.
> And more than anything else I'm sad.
> And not just now – not just right now.
> But all the time.
>
> …

BEA. I didn't know things were so hard for you.

> …
>
> Your… life… is very far away from mine.

VEDA. Because we don't really know each other.

BEA. Doesn't bother me.

VEDA. Okay.

BEA. V, I don't have time for your feelings being bigger than mine any more.

VEDA. They never have been.

BEA. You put yourself first.

VEDA. Someone has to.

BEA. Not in my home.

VEDA. It was ours once.

BEA. But you left.

VEDA. I was a child.

BEA. But you never really came back.

VEDA. I tried.

BEA. Not hard enough.

VEDA. Because you turned it into a – a –

BEA. I just stayed put.

VEDA. And got gobbled up by it, like everything gets gobbled up by this – this – this – I am not going to leave you like this again.

BEA. It's not a one-day job.

VEDA. I do love you.

BEA. No.
No.
You have pretended I don't exist for years.
So, no.

VEDA. I never pretended you didn't exist – that would've been a real luxury.

BEA. True to form, you scuttled away.

VEDA. You keyed a cock-and-balls on my bonnet.

BEA. It was a middle finger.

VEDA. It wasn't.

BEA. That's how it started.

VEDA. Doesn't matter how it started.

BEA. It actually does.

VEDA. Then it started with you ploughing through a version of Dad's eulogy that I did NOT sign off on, without letting me say a word, while I stood up there next to you like a fucking chump.

BEA. Because you were an absolute bloody delight that day?

VEDA. I never said I / was –

BEA. / You drank half a bottle of wine and said that when I get crushed to death in here you'll burn the whole house down like the big fat mum in *What's Gilbert Grape Eating?*

VEDA. It's *What's Eating Gilbert Grape*.

BEA. Everyone heard.

...

You fucked up my last few months with him.

VEDA. That wasn't about you, it was about this house, this house wasn't fit for purpose.

BEA. They prodded and poked and ticked boxes on clipboards / and –

VEDA. / And did nothing.

BEA. Because they saw how well looked after he was.

But you still made sure everyone at the wake heard about my filthy-fucking-deathtrap-house.

VEDA. Imagine – just imagine – for a moment – the conversations I had to have with Ash.

BEA. That's being a mum.

VEDA. What do you know about being a mum?

BEA. After – I made it very clear that I wanted a relationship with Ash.

VEDA. Because you pick and choose your favourites – pit people against each other.

BEA. I have bent over backwards to make / everything alright always.

VEDA. / There was more to do.

BEA. It was your turn, Veda.

...

It was your turn to do the fixing.

VEDA. My turn?

BEA. I'd done more than my fair share.

VEDA. Because we all had to wait for you / to be –

BEA. / Because I put the most in / always –

VEDA. / No one could try without you flinching / or – or –

BEA. / Because you don't know how to care for things without –

VEDA. Without what?

BEA. Nothing

VEDA. What?

BEA. Leave it.

VEDA. No. What?

BEA. You break everything.

…

You break everything.

…

Even now, you can't just be sorry, can you?

VEDA. I'm here.

BEA. You're a bit late.

VEDA. Not too late.
Not yet.
And I am sorry.
…

I am sorry.
Because it does matter what starts it.
Doesn't it?
What starts it always matters.
But I want to fucking fix it.
Because I'm ill and my life is its own pile of shit right now and I'd rather be at your throat here than playing out being at your throat in my head all day every day.

BEA. You're ill?

VEDA *nods*.

What kind?

VEDA. Of ill?

BEA. Yes.

VEDA. Not a very forgiving kind.

BEA. Shit.

VEDA. Is a bit.

BEA. What is it?

VEDA. I want to do the least damage to Ash.

BEA. You're scaring me.

VEDA. They're still doing lots of tests.

BEA. For?

VEDA. Fucking enigma code.

BEA. Is it…?

VEDA. I don't know.

BEA. How long have you known?

VEDA. A while.

BEA. What's that?

VEDA. A few months.

BEA. Does Ash know?

VEDA. Yes.

BEA. And how is he?

VEDA. I don't know.

BEA. But how – how does he seem?

VEDA. I just want to do the least damage.

BEA. Okay.

VEDA. It started with these headaches – head-in-a-vice headaches.
And this wobbliness.
This lack of focus.
With sheet music, I had to close one eye just to…
Course in the great tradition of our family I tried my best to ignore them.
Then I had the first seizure in assembly bashing out 'Cauliflowers Fluffy'.

BEA (*singing*). Cauliflowers fluffy and cabbages green,
Strawberries sweeter than I've ever –
FUCK

VEDA. Fuck indeed.

BEA. You used to have febrile convulsions.

VEDA. Don't think it's linked.

BEA. I can still see Dad running downstairs with you in his arms – stiff as a board.

VEDA. Whatever it turns out to be, it's quite serious, it's serious.

BEA. …Do they hurt?

VEDA. What?

BEA. Seizures?

VEDA. Not in the moment but after… it's like someone's unplugged you then jammed the plug back into a live socket and there's this soreness – this surge.

BEA. I don't like you being in pain.

…

So that's why you've come?

VEDA. It's part of it.

BEA. Okay?

VEDA. The big bit is I'm scared.

BEA. Oh.

VEDA. And every time I've been really scared you've been there.

...

And you –
You have this warmth.
And it frightens me.
You are the warmest person I have ever known.
And I want a bit of it.

BEA. I'm sorry you're ill.

VEDA. But?

BEA. There's no but.

VEDA. I know it's not fair, it isn't fair for me to –

BEA. I'm just still really cross.

VEDA. I know you are.
I know.
How could you not be?
You've swallowed everything down.
Done your best to be everything I haven't been.
And that is what has fucking shackled you.

BEA. I'm not shackled.

VEDA. Aren't you?
Look.
Look, Bea.
Not at me.
At this.
This is the shell you crawled into when / Mum –

BEA. / I don't want to do this.

VEDA. Course you don't.

BEA. You don't get to turn up here and make me do this just because you're ~~ill~~.

VEDA. But I'm going to anyway.

BEA. It's in my make-up.

VEDA. No you're better than this.

BEA. Are you going to get better?

VEDA. I'd really like to.

BEA. But really?

   VEDA *nods*.

VEDA. What is it they do with trees?
   Count the rings and you'll know how old it is?
   Split this place down the middle and you'd count ring after ring of –
   We didn't cope.
   Hey?

BEA. Is that what you see?

VEDA. I want better for Ash.

BEA. He's different.

VEDA. He's not.

BEA. He's brilliant.

VEDA. I don't think I like him.

   BEA *retreats*.

   He's this unfurling thing.
   He won't –
   He doesn't –
   He barely leaves his room.
   And he doesn't know that I know that he's in some weird online game relationship with someone who apparently lives in Tampa-fucking-Florida who's almost certainly a paedophile – because I don't know what to do and Sid won't do anything unless it involves a pneumatic drill and a spirit level.

BEA. How long has that been going on for?

VEDA. He's like a woodlouse.

BEA. How long?

VEDA. I don't know, he won't talk to me – when I try to talk to him he grows spikes.

BEA. Then be gentle.

VEDA. I'm not a gentle person.

BEA. Pretend to be.

VEDA. I think you'd like him.

BEA. I love him.

VEDA. He has a bonsai.

BEA. Yeah?

VEDA. Yeah.

BEA. I love a bonsai.

VEDA. I know.
He's given it a name and everything.

BEA. What's he called it?

VEDA.… Can't remember.

BEA *deflates*.

How is work?

BEA. Fine.

VEDA. Really?

BEA. As long as you stay out of the politics and the in-fighting.

VEDA. Still that bad?

BEA. It's actually turned into a really nice little garden centre – a real hive.

VEDA. Good.

BEA. What kind of bonsai is it?

VEDA. Don't know.

BEA. Japanese maple?

VEDA. Don't think so.

BEA. Fern pine?

VEDA. Doesn't ring a bell.

BEA. Chinese elm? Japanese flowering cherry?

VEDA. Firing them off like that doesn't help.

BEA. Who got it for him?

VEDA. He did.

BEA. Is it green-leafed? Red-leafed? Does it flower? Is it upright? Does it lean? One trunk? Two?

VEDA. You know you're really irritating when you know something that someone else doesn't.

BEA. You could just say if it's green.

VEDA. Yes, Bea, it's green. It looks like a tiny, old-man-looking tree. And the bark is all craggy like, like, like a ballsack.

BEA. Sounds a lot like a Juniper.

VEDA. That's it! I can see the little carboard thingy.

BEA. You've never been green-thumbed.

VEDA. You're forgetting Margaret, my cactus!

BEA. I think you're forgetting Margaret – died young, victim of neglect!

VEDA. He could be a really nice and good person.

BEA. Okay.

VEDA. He takes his bonsai out into the garden when it's warm and sunny.
And I wish he was little again.

…

BEA. You warm yet?

VEDA. A bit.

BEA. Hot squash?

VEDA. No.

BEA. It's blackcurrant, no apple.

VEDA. It's alright.

BEA. Could make us some chamomile?

VEDA. You hate chamomile.

BEA. I know, tastes like bathwater, but you like it so…

VEDA. Hot squash please.

BEA. Hot squash it is.

> BEA *takes a bottle of water from a cupboard to fill the kettle.*

VEDA. Did anything more happen with that nice man from the café at the garden centre?

BEA. Nope.

> BEA *climbs up onto the arm of the armchair to reach a kettle on a shelf.*

VEDA. He came to the wake, I thought you were…

BEA. He was representing the garden centre.

VEDA. I liked his hair.

BEA. No you didn't.

VEDA. No I didn't.

BEA. He's – sorry, don't move, the weight has to –

VEDA. So nothing's ever going to happen with the nice man from the café at the garden centre then?

BEA. Probably not.

VEDA. That's sad, Bea.

> BEA *fills the kettle.*

BEA. You're taking it harder than me.

BEA switches on the kettle.

He does – no – it's silly / it's –

VEDA. What?

BEA. He still wraps up one of them fancy jammy dodgers and puts it in my cubby hole at the end of his shift if there's one left.

VEDA. That's… lovely.

The kettle boils.

BEA. He is lovely.

Something HUGE dawns on VEDA.

VEDA. FUCK.

BEA. What?

VEDA. Fuck.

BEA. WHAT?

VEDA (*standing*). Where are the stairs?

The armchair wobbles as the weight shifts and BEA loses her balance.

As BEA tumbles:

Where are the fucking stairs?   BEA. I said DON'T –

BEA lands on the floor.

As she does, VEDA *moves out of her way and steps into a bucket full of soaking cutlery.*

HOLY MOTHER OF ~~FUCK~~

BEA. My bloody back.

VEDA. What's even…?

VEDA pulls her foot out of the bucket.

A fork hangs out of her foot.

BEA. VEDA, STAY VERY STILL.

VEDA. IT'S NOT A FUCKING BEAR IT'S A FORK.

BEA. THERE'S A FOOT IN YOUR FORK.

VEDA. THERE'S A FORK IN MY FOOT.

BEA. Oh my God there's A FORK IN YOUR FOOT.

VEDA reaches down to her foot.

DON'T.

VEDA grabs hold of the fork and pulls it out.

You're a fucking champ.

VEDA. Get a towel.

BEA. Is there much blood?

VEDA. No, there's water all over your carpet.

BEA. I've got plasters and bandages / and –

VEDA (*inspecting her foot*). / I'm not –

BEA. I've got wound dressings!

VEDA. I'm not bleeding.

BEA. What?

VEDA. It's not – my sock came off worst.

BEA. That can be darned.

VEDA. Fuck darning.

BEA. Show me.

VEDA. Barely broke the skin.

BEA. Show me.

VEDA sticks out her foot to BEA.

Maybe you've traumatised it.

VEDA. What?

BEA. It can happen.

I traumatised my heel once – I stepped on a pine cone barefoot and that did it – they can be sharp.

VEDA. Your back okay?

BEA. It's my bulging disc.

VEDA. They're gone aren't they?

BEA. What are?

VEDA. The stairs.
They've been... absorbed.
What about upstairs?
Can you even...?

BEA. If you know how.

VEDA. This really is it, isn't it.
This is all the space you have left.

BEA. It's all I need.

VEDA. Where do you cook?

BEA. I eat, V.

VEDA. Where do you wash?

BEA. I'm a clean person.

VEDA. That's not what I asked.

BEA. I clean myself.
I clean my home.
I am a clean person.

VEDA. I didn't think it could get worse, like it was always the worst it could be, that way it could get better.

BEA. So I've exceeded your expectations?

VEDA envelops BEA in an almighty hug.

It lasts for a little while before:

Ow.

VEDA. Sorry.

BEA. It's my coccyx, I need to –

BEA lies down on the floor to stretch.

VEDA. Sore?

BEA. I shouldn't really complain.

VEDA. Why not?

BEA holds her hand out to VEDA.

BEA. Come here.

VEDA. Budge up then.

BEA shuffles.

BEA. It towers.

VEDA lies down next to her.

VEDA. I feel very small.

BEA. It's like looking up from the bottom of a well.

VEDA notices the fork that was impaled in her foot on the floor.

VEDA. Isn't your best fork, is it?

BEA. No.

VEDA. What were you doing with a bucket of soapy cutlery?

BEA. They were soaking.

VEDA. Big banquet planned?

BEA. What do you think?

I picked them up this morning in the Shelter shop.

VEDA. And what makes them so special?

BEA. They're not all that special.

VEDA. But why do you like them?

BEA. They're Viner's.
　The Country Garden set.
　Or most of a set.
　Mum had the same one.
　It was a gift from Nanny.
　It's upstairs.
　The original that is.
　The box was lined with this appley green velvety felt stuff.
　Like a smart little briefcase for cutlery.
　So when I saw these in town it felt like it could be a kind of sister set.

VEDA. I feel a few forks short of a set sometimes.

BEA. That's one way of putting it.

VEDA. I don't recognise the pattern.

BEA. No?

VEDA. No.

BEA. You never did help with the washing-up.

VEDA. That's why I married Sid – the one thing he's good at.

BEA. Remember how Mum used to dip each piece of cutlery into Goddard's Silver Dip?

VEDA. Slowly poisoning us.

　BEA *whacks* VEDA.

BEA. Don't say that!　　　　　　VEDA. Ow!

VEDA. Do you think she actually liked doing any of it?

BEA. Those were her ways.

VEDA. But did she like it?

BEA. I think / she quite –

VEDA. / She just regurgitated the nineteen-fucking-fifties.

BEA. Don't be nasty.

VEDA. I'm not being nasty.

BEA. You will be if you don't stop where you are.

VEDA *surrenders*.

Is Sid looking after you?

VEDA. He's started whittling.

BEA. He hasn't?

VEDA. He did me a squirrel.

BEA. I suppose that's quite nice.

VEDA. It is quite nice.

…

But Ash isn't going to cope if he just has his dad.

BEA. You're not going to.

VEDA. But he won't.
He'll turn in on himself.
And I think he'll get angry.
Or vacant.
Or both.
I don't really know.
But he doesn't really like the world – not enough to go out into it any more – and that'll get worse – it'll get worse when things get worse.

…

I want you in Ash's life.

BEA. Alright.

VEDA. Is it?

BEA. It's what I've always wanted.

VEDA. Good.

BEA. He still got braces?

VEDA. No, they've come off.

BEA. Good.

VEDA. I thought it'd give him a bit of a boost but...
You'll look after him?

BEA. I said so.

VEDA. I do like him.
I like him very much.
I love him very much.

BEA. I know.

VEDA. So you have got to be better than this.

BEA *bristles*.

I mean it.

Because he is gentle and gorgeous and brainy and kind.

The air in the room turns thick.

I won't leave you at the bottom of the well.

BEA *furls*.

BEA. It's embarrassing.

...

Does he know that I live like this?

VEDA. Ash?

BEA. Does he know what I'm like?

VEDA. Some of it.

BEA. He mustn't see it.
He mustn't see it.
He mustn't.

VEDA. He remembers an Aladdin's cave.
In the backseat of the car he used to plead to come in with me.

BEA. All the neighbours think I'm normal.

VEDA. Oh Bea.

BEA. It feels like a big trick.

VEDA. Does anyone else know?

BEA. No.
    No one.
    No one knows.
    Apart from you.
    And Dad.
    He lived in it.

VEDA. He did more than live in it.

BEA. I would've always been like this.

VEDA. You don't really believe that?

BEA. There's a fault line ~~in me~~.

VEDA. No.

BEA. I'm so embarrassed.

VEDA. You're not faulty.

VEDA cosmically urges BEA to open herself up.

BEA. The other night – the other night – you remember Jan next door – well – she locked herself out doing the bins. She was sat on her front step in her nightie… shivering. I went out, and I asked if she was alright, and if she needed me to do something. Her mobile was in her bedside drawer inside. So, I called her daughter Cheryl, because we exchanged numbers after Jan had her fall. Anyway, she's sat outside in the cold, and she tells me she's cold, and if she can come in here. But she doesn't know I live like this. And she can't know. So I had to say no. I gave her a big fleece and a blanket, and I sat out with her. But I couldn't let her in.

VEDA. You sat with her and you kept her warm.

BEA. But it isn't enough.

VEDA. It's more than a lot of people would do.

BEA. It's not good enough.

VEDA. Bea, you treat cutlery with more care than I've ever treated / people.

BEA. / Had that been Dad out / there –

VEDA. / You didn't treat her unkindly.

BEA. She could've caught pneumonia.

VEDA. But she didn't.

BEA. She had pleurisy twice last year.

VEDA. And still going strong.

BEA. Ish.

VEDA. Still going strong-ish.

BEA. I did give her my best blanket.

VEDA. There you go.

BEA. I told her I was in the middle of recarpeting.

VEDA. You said what you could.

BEA. I lied.

VEDA. It isn't that simple.

BEA. You're being too nice to me.

VEDA. Doesn't sound like me.

BEA. I have something of yours.

VEDA. I think you have lots of things that were mine.

BEA. Wait there!

BEA disappears down the narrow corridor.

VEDA. Oh Bea.

BEA drags in an electric keyboard.

BEA. Ta-dah!

VEDA. I made you sell that.

BEA. I know! I set up another account on eBay to buy it from myself!

VEDA. I don't remember it so... square and... bulky.

BEA. Don't you?

VEDA. And I was a lot smaller back then.

BEA. It's memories.

VEDA. My wild youth.

BEA. Whenever I touch those keys, they still feel warm.

VEDA. Does she still work?

BEA. Oh yeah.

VEDA. Plug her in.

BEA *does*.

Remember the one I had with the multicoloured keys? Blue, yellow, pink... purple, green, mint.

BEA. I got a shitty recorder the same year.

VEDA *turns the keyboard on*.

Play something.

VEDA *prepares with the flourish of a concert pianist*.

Play the really fast one, you know the one –

VEDA. I know the one.

BEA. Dad loved that one.

VEDA *goes cold*.

She turns the keyboard off.

What?

VEDA. I don't want to.

BEA. Are you for / real?

VEDA. / I don't want to any more.

BEA. Fine.

VEDA. You shouldn't have kept it – sold it and rebought it – whatever you did – you shouldn't've.

...

BEA. I thought you'd like it.

...

...

...

VEDA *turns the keyboard on.*

She presses a button and a demo track plays.

She presses more buttons trying to find BEA*'s favourite.*

She finds it.

She wiggles.

Then, BEA *wiggles.*

The demo track ends abruptly.

It's the best thing in this whole house.

VEDA. Everything is the best thing in this house to you.
You sit in his old camping chair for God's sake.
The legs are bent.
The pattern's faded.
But you worship it.

BEA. It reminds me.

VEDA. Of what?

BEA. Holidays.

VEDA. Camping three and half miles down the road?

BEA. Us together.

VEDA. Two weeks of warm apple juice and not shitting.

BEA. Of Frazzles for breakfast, lunch and tea.

VEDA. Of trapped sheep projectile shitting in campsite showers.

BEA. Dad saved that sheep.

VEDA. He didn't.

BEA. He did.

VEDA. That sheep died in there.

BEA. He definitely saved at least one sheep.

VEDA. We didn't grow up in *All Creatures Great and*-fucking-*Small*.

BEA. I love that chair.

VEDA. It's tat.

BEA. It's him.

VEDA. It's not.
And that keyboard isn't me.
It isn't me.
But you chose it over actual me.
You chose all of this over actual – over the people who – and he made you like this.

BEA. No.

VEDA. He did.

BEA. You're wrong.

VEDA. He mopped up your grief and soaked you both in it.

BEA. He didn't do this.

VEDA. He fucking did.

BEA. You buggered off.

VEDA. I was always going to leave when I did.

BEA. Mum had only just gone.

VEDA. It was months later.

BEA. We were still saying goodbye.

VEDA. So was I.

BEA. You couldn't wait to leave.

VEDA. You and Dad left me out.

BEA. Bullshit.

VEDA. You had this private little world that I was too big for.

BEA. You didn't try,

VEDA. It hurt too much.

BEA. You barely ever came home.

VEDA. I came home.

BEA. First couple of years after maybe.

VEDA. That was enough.

BEA. You'd had enough of us?

VEDA. It was the way you –
You clung on to everything.
Her things.
Then, things that looked like her things.
Then, feathers and crap you'd collect off the street.
When a blouse stopped smelling like her – or a conker started rotting you'd have these tantrums – this panic that just didn't stop –
But he let you run this house like she did so nothing changed for him.

BEA. You looked after yourself.

VEDA. The first time I came home – the way you and Dad – you kissed the photos of her in the hall goodnight.

BEA. I needed that.

VEDA. That whole weekend I sat on the stairs and watched your… ways… you laying a place for Mum at the table.

BEA. Dad needed that.

VEDA. He needed you.

BEA. It was a moment of a time that / was –

VEDA. A moment?

BEA. A moment.

VEDA. It's everything.

BEA. I grew out of it.

VEDA. There were things you could've done.

BEA. I've done lots of things.

VEDA. You had things to leave for.

BEA. I didn't want to go.

VEDA. There were things you deserved to do.

BEA. Things you forced me to do, and I tried them all and I hated them all.

VEDA. You were at university less than a term.

BEA. Yes and I hated it.

VEDA. No, you couldn't be away from this fucking house.

BEA. Dad didn't choose to not cope.

VEDA. I think that's exactly what he did.

BEA. You think that because you're not a nice person so you don't see the world or anyone else as nice.

VEDA. I've been thinking about Patrick a lot.

BEA *falters*.

I think about Patrick quite a lot actually.
I think about him asking you to live with him and you telling him you couldn't leave Dad.

BEA. Dad needed a support.

VEDA. That's not how you choose who to spend your life with.

BEA. Dad needed my help.

VEDA. He made sure that was clear every time anything good came your way.

BEA. It was me caring for him or a stranger caring for him.

VEDA. Wouldn't have been a stranger after a while.

BEA. What do you mean 'made sure' of it?

VEDA. No coincidence that every time something good threatened to take you away he ended up in hospital hypo-fucking-glycaemic on insulin strike.

BEA *remembers*.

For all the good in him – because I saw some of that too – he used you.

BEA. Every time I left him, even just for a night, I couldn't bear making him so lonely.

VEDA. He shouldn't've needed you like he did.

BEA. That's grief.

VEDA. But he held you there with him.
And he took chunks out of you.
And when I first held Ash, these images – thoughts – I don't know what – but my mouth was full of blood and there was just this big chunk out of him – like I had to stuff mouthfuls of him into me – and then when I saw you – I saw all the chunks Dad took out of you.

BEA. You make him sound / like a – a –

VEDA. /I want to squeeze him out of you because you're like an – an – an – abscess that just / won't –

BEA. Abscess?

VEDA. No – I just –

BEA. Abscess?

VEDA. Yes.

BEA. The way you speak is…

VEDA. I want – have wanted – you to just burst and leak and and and drain – just empty yourself of this – because that closeness – it – did something to me – and – and – and I am sorry –
I am sorry.
I am sorry because I got out.
And you didn't.
And I left you there…
And it was really hard to put everything into pulling you out when you made it look like you wanted it.

BEA. I made choices.

VEDA. I know.

BEA. As an adult, I made choices.

VEDA. I understand.

BEA. And sometimes it's like the things I wanted to do, I have kind of done.
Like I feel like I have parented.
Like I parented a parent.
Like I –
Once, I was getting Dad into the shower, and I plonked him down on the shower stool, and there was this crunch. I'd sat him down on his comb. The tortoiseshell one he'd always had. And a few prongs snapped off. And his bum cheek was bleeding. Three little punctures. I had to bend him over the chair and pick the little shards out. And he giggled. He just kept giggling. Like a baby.

VEDA. I'm sorry I left you with that.

BEA. Dabbing Savlon on his bum was a privilege.

…

You look at me so…

VEDA. What?

BEA. …with so much…

VEDA waits.

It's not pity.
It's not that simple.
But it makes my skin itch.
And I have tried to make that look change, to make it something different, but it's beyond me.
Because you are ashamed of me.

VEDA *approaches* BEA.

She plants an enormous kiss on her cheek.

VEDA. I am not ashamed of you.
I have been embarrassed.
It has been embarrassing.
And I think it is a huge shame that you haven't been able to be the monumental person you are.
But I am not ashamed of you.

BEA. Really?

VEDA. Yes.

BEA. I almost found someone to talk about it all with.

VEDA. Did you?

BEA. But I couldn't do it.
I started watching this programme.
About this kind of thing.
And I kept thinking wow that's disgusting, I'm not that bad, am I?
But I am that bad.
And I felt disgusting.
And every time the cleaning team picked something up – or moved something – there was more filth under it… Fresh fucking hell. And you're there, having to watch people in white masks treat the things that are so precious to you like biohazard.
So I didn't go to the appointment.

VEDA. No one was going to make you do a documentary.

BEA. But they might look at me like that.

VEDA. The only person I'm – I'm ashamed of me.

BEA. What?

VEDA. It took me looking at Ash and seeing you in him to really give a shit.

BEA. He won't end up like this.

VEDA. But beware the quiet child.
Beware the affable child.
Beware the kid who takes themselves off to their room to feel how they feel because there is chaos inside of them and that chaos – the second they don't have a purpose – they'll rupture.

BEA. You won't let that happen.

VEDA. And neither will you.

BEA. Or Sid.

VEDA. I think the best thing about Sid is that Ash could fucking... skin cats... or fuck a sheep... and he's so immovable so tunnel vision that he'd rock up to prison and witter with him about tongue-and-groove joints.

But he'd never think to ask why.

BEA. He'll / do –

VEDA. / I had sex with a horrible man from a horrible app.

BEA. You didn't.

VEDA. It was awful.

BEA. Why?

VEDA. I wanted to be touched like I wasn't ill.

BEA. Oh.

VEDA. Turns out a bottle of blush rosé and two fingers while your husband is passed out downstairs like a slug in slippers is the better deal.

BEA *laughs*.

VEDA *laughs too.*

They laugh together.

What do you want?

BEA. What?

VEDA. What do you want?

BEA *thinks.*

WHAT DO YOU WANT?

BEA. A dog.

VEDA. What?

BEA. I want a dog.

VEDA. Really?

BEA. Yes I want a dog because I want to live in a house where I can have a dog without worrying it'd die trapped under god-knows-what-shite.

VEDA. What kind?

BEA. I don't mind – I don't – a little mutt maybe – maybe a bit of Schnauzer thrown in – the ones with the eyebrows and moustaches.

VEDA. I can see that for you.

BEA. I'd like to wake up in bed to a little dog licking my face with his lead in his mouth and his – it's stupid.

VEDA. It isn't.

BEA. I wake up in that chair, V, and some days, I have these days when –
Days when I'm just full of the idea that I can do something. And it lasts for a bit –
Just for a bit before it goes.
Some days, I think that a fire or a flood would be a VERY BRILLIANT THING.
Or a VERY PRECISE plane crash.

Something to annihilate the problem.
The only problem with that is that I know that BRILLIANT FEELING wouldn't last.
I'd jump straight into the carnage.
Walk into the flames
Or the waves
Or the wreck
Because I wouldn't be able to help myself.
I'd drown, or I'd burn trying to choose what to save
I'd get SO STUCK
And everything would cave in on me
And I'd be crushed under cookbooksandArgoscataloguesandradiosandcutleryandeveryTVI'veeverowned
or –
or –
or –

VEDA. Or not.
Or not.

BEA. No?

VEDA. No.
Because you're hardy.

BEA. I'm hardy?

VEDA. Sturdy.

BEA. Robust.

VEDA. You withstand.

BEA. I'd like to lift this house over my head and just throw it so far.

VEDA. And you could.

BEA. I'd go with it.

VEDA. No.

BEA. I'd go with it, I would.

ACT ONE, SCENE ONE 49

VEDA. If a sinkhole opened up beneath this house you wouldn't sink with it.

BEA. I wouldn't stand a chance.

VEDA. You can't be sunk.
You can't be sunk, Bea.
Not by the weight of this place.

BEA. So what do I do?
What do you want me to do at the bottom of a fucking sinkhole?

VEDA. Dig your fucking fingers in.

BEA. That easy?

VEDA. No.
It's not easy at all.
But you sink your fingers and your nails into the gravel and the soil and the sand and you –

BEA. Slip.

VEDA. So you bite down with your razor-sharp teeth into the earth and you climb and climb and / climb.

BEA. / And when my foot slips in the slurry / and I –

VEDA. You climb.

BEA. And climb.

VEDA. And fucking climb.

BEA. And when the pipes burst and the water floods in?

VEDA. You don't choke.

BEA. Because I can breathe.

VEDA. You can breathe
Because you have fucking gills now
And you propel yourself to the surface

BEA. And when I get there?

VEDA. The surface breaks
   And the light hits
   Like a fucking wall
   And you are unsinkable
   Do you hear me?
   You are unsinkable.

BEA. It'll all be gone.

VEDA. It disappears.

BEA. It won't come back.

VEDA. Do you want it back?

BEA. It buries itself.

VEDA. But not you.

BEA. No, not me.

VEDA. Because every brilliant bit of you adapts to withstand every shitty thing that's happened to you.

BEA. And I'm hardy.

VEDA. Sturdy.

BEA. Robust.

VEDA. Muscular.

BEA. And I have fucking gills for some reason too.

VEDA. And what'll you do?

BEA. I don't know.

VEDA. What do you want to do?

BEA. Just be with you.

VEDA. And what do we do?

BEA. You know.

> VEDA *turns the keyboard back on.*
>
> *She prepares to play with great flourish.*

ACT ONE, SCENE ONE   51

She plays a note over and over again as she increases the volume.

She starts playing then something ELECTRIC AND MONUMENTAL takes over.

The world vibrates and pulses to a song like 'Because the Night' by Patti Smith.

BEA *dances.*

VEDA *gets up – the music continues.*

They dance together.

The vibrations of the music swell.

The house trembles.

Something falls.

A tear in the ceiling appears.

The music gets louder.

The sisters dance harder.

They invite destruction.

VEDA. Isn't it BRILLIANT?

BEA *dances, sweats, ruptures.*

MY BRILLIANT, BRILLIANT LITTLE SISTER.

The tear in the ceiling opens.

A myriad of objects falls on BEA *and* VEDA.

Both sisters are buried underneath an enormous pile of possessions.

ACT TWO

Scene One

A hospital.

ASH *stands at the end of* BEA*'s bed.*

ASH. Dad's looking for free parking.

BEA. But he's seen her?
  …
  You've seen her?
  …
  Ash?

  ASH *shakes his head.*

  But she's here?

  ASH *shakes his head.*

  No, she has to be.
  …
  Ash?

ASH. Yeah?

BEA. Ash.

ASH. Aunty Bea?

BEA. Where is she?
No one will tell me.

ASH. They… can't.

BEA. What?

ASH. She's not here.

BEA. But you are?

ASH. Because you're here.

BEA. But she was with me.

   ASH *falters*.

   She held my hand.

   ASH *flounders*.

   She held my hand.

   ASH *shakes his head*.

   There was something pressing – pressing here – pressing here on my chest and she – she – she – she found my – my – your cheeks.

   ASH *squirms*.

   You're leaking.

ASH. I'm not.

   ASH *coils inside*.

   BEA *tries to sit up*.

BEA. Remember your grandpa used to say that?

   ASH *nods*.

   That's what he always said.

   BEA *sits up*.

ASH. Aunty Bea.

BEA. You're massive.

   BEA *is woozy*.

ASH. Steady.

   ASH *steadies* BEA.

BEA. Got to dry those up.

   ASH *flinches*.

Those cheeks always turn into beetroots before the tears come.

BEA *points to her eye, then her heart, then to* ASH, *who doesn't understand.*

I do.
I love you.

ASH. It's... something happened.

A sharp pain shoots through BEA.

You okay?

BEA *winces.*

You're not.

BEA. I need to see her.

ASH. You can't.

BEA. She was talking.
She was talking to me.
She kept talking to me.

ASH. She didn't.

BEA. You weren't there.

ASH. She wasn't there.

BEA. No listen – she was with me yesterday – of all the days – she was with me.

ASH. Where?

BEA. At the house.

...

She was stood on the doorstep.
Soaked.
She was standing there.
Soaked through.
I felt her.

ASH. Not yesterday.

BEA. Yes yesterday.

ASH. NO.

BEA. Is she… very hurt?

ASH. Don't make me.

BEA. I want her.
I want her here.

ASH. I don't want to.

BEA. You can.

ASH. But you're not okay.

BEA. I am.

ASH. You're not.
It's… not.

BEA. What's not?

ASH. What happened.

BEA. It's okay.

ASH. It's NOT.

BEA. Is she…?

ASH becomes horribly adult.

BEA looks up at/to him.

ASH. She's… um… it's like I said… Mum's… she's not here.

BEA. What do you mean not here?

ASH. I mean she's not here… not any more… she's not here any more.

BEA's world spasms.

And she wasn't with you yesterday – it's not – she wasn't – that's not true – because – in the morning – yesterday morning – there was water – there was water coming through the ceiling – before college – water – so I went upstairs – and the door was locked – so I couldn't –

BEA. No.

ASH. A seizure – in the shower.

BEA. No, no, no, no, you have to tell the truth.

> ASH *is stunned*.

Because that's not the truth.

> ASH *is winded*.

You're not telling the truth, you have to tell the –

ASH. I'm / not –

BEA. / You're lying.

ASH. I'm –

BEA. Because she was as real to me yesterday as you are now.

> ASH *recoils*.

She told me about you.	
She did.	
And you –	ASH. Stop.
She played the keyboard.	
And she told me you –	
She told me you have a – a – a –	Please stop.

BEA. No you have to listen to me you have to –

ASH. DON'T.

> ASH *retreats*.

BEA. Don't go.

ASH. Why're you doing this?

BEA. I'm not –

ASH. Why are you making me do this?

BEA. Don't leave I need to remember I can't remember what I needed to remember what she said –

ASH. Don't come fucking near me
　Don't
　DON'T
　YOU'RE –

BEA. BONSAI!

　ASH *falters*.

　Bonsai
　Bonsai
　Bonsai
　BONSAI –

　ASH *shakes his head*.

ASH. She was right about you.

BEA. She told me.

　ASH *grabs his things and leaves*.

　Alone, BEA *shatters*.

　Oh Veda, Veda, Veda, Veda, Veda, what have you done?

Scene Two

A few weeks later.

In BEA*'s ruptured house.*

ASH, *wearing a smart black suit, stands alone and takes in the carnage.*

BEA (*hidden*). ITOLDYOUTOFUCKOFFYESTERDAY

　ASH *jumps*.

　He turns around.

ASH. I wasn't –

BEA *appears.*

She sees ASH.

She softens.

BEA. It's you.

ASH. You're not coming.

BEA. You scared me.

ASH. You're not coming.

BEA. You scared me – I thought you were the kids from down the road.

ASH. What?

BEA. They got in when I was in hospital.

ASH. What're you doing here?

BEA. They're always drinking cider outside Co-op.

…

ASH. Why aren't you coming?

BEA. I'm just saying so you know if you find a used condom or a baggie it's not mine it's theirs.

ASH. They had sex in here?

BEA. Desperate times.

ASH. Yeah.

BEA. And no, I'm not coming, they'll sniff this place out the second it's empty.

…

ASH. I don't feel sorry for you.

BEA. Didn't ask you to.

ASH. Dad said you wouldn't come.

BEA. Did he?

ASH. Said it'd take fucking Time Team to dig you out.

BEA. Is that what you've come to do?

ASH. No.

BEA. Good.

ASH. This isn't about you.

BEA. Okay.

ASH. It isn't.

BEA. So why are you here?

ASH. Because you've made it about you.

BEA. You should go.

ASH. I'm not leaving.

BEA. Does your dad know you're here?

ASH. Course not.

BEA. Go.

ASH. Can't.

BEA. Go.

ASH. Next bus isn't for an hour.

BEA. What?

ASH. It's one-a-fucking-hour.

BEA. But it starts / at –

ASH. / I know when it starts.

...

So I know I've sort of already missed it.

...

I've already missed it.

BEA. No.

ASH. We've both missed it.

BEA. No you can get the X3 / to –

ASH. / You've made me miss it.

BEA. The X3 / will take you to –

ASH. / I've missed / it.

BEA. / And if you change at the park-and-ride / you can –

ASH. / Might as well fucking walk it from / there.

BEA. / Tell your dad to come get / you.

ASH. / This morning – fucking crack of dawn – and it's you – you're the thing I'm thinking about – seeing you – or not seeing you – you turning up for Mum – is the thing I have to think about.

BEA. I didn't / want –

ASH. / You've made me look for you.

BEA *recoils*.

Have you been there before?
Have you seen the place where they're doing it?

BEA *shakes her head*.

It's bleak.
It's a fucking brick bungalow in a carpark in the middle of bumfucknowhere.

BEA. Ash.

ASH. It says there's a garden.
There's not a garden.
I couldn't find a garden.
I found a patch of grass with a shitty little stone fountain that wasn't even on.
It's shit.
It's really shit there.

BEA. That's just what they're like.

ASH. No, this one's the shittest.

BEA. Is it?

ASH. Yeah.

BEA. Alright.

ASH. Looks out onto the power station.
You know the one that collapsed and killed those people?

BEA. Just awful.

ASH. I keep thinking about the people that died there because they can't have been cremated at the place where Mum's – because it's right fucking there staring them in the face – I don't know what Mum thought about nuclear energy.

BEA *is lost*.

Do you?

BEA. I don't know.

ASH. She hated the green food bin.

BEA. Course she did.

ASH. She forgot to put a bag-liner thing in it one time when Dad was away for like a week so she threw the whole bin out.

BEA. That sounds like her.

…

ASH. I'm not not-there because I don't want to be – not because I'm scared or –

BEA. It's alright to be –

ASH. I'm not there because I don't know what the point is because no one else wants to be there and if you get to not be there then FUCK IT so do I.

BEA. Don't raise / your voice.

ASH. / I'm not like you, you know.

BEA. I didn't say you were.

ASH. I'm actually a really strong person.

BEA. God that sounds tiring.

ASH. The place where Grandpa… was a lot nicer.
I remember it nicer.

BEA. That one had a nice little garden.

ASH. That's where I got put with Dad.

BEA. There were wind chimes.

ASH. I don't know what it's like inside.
Not when it's happening.
Mum didn't let me… be in there.

BEA. You were too young.

ASH. She let me in the church.

BEA. It's different.
It's softer.

ASH. Softer?

BEA. It can be.

ASH. It wasn't.

BEA. Softer not… not easier… not less…

ASH. You didn't let Mum read what I'd written.

BEA. What?

ASH. Mum wanted to read something I'd written for Grandpa but you just went on and on and / on –

BEA. / I didn't know.

ASH. I'd never seen Mum that sad before.

…

I was there in the car watching your screaming match in the carpark after Grandpa's – we were leaving – and she told me to get in the car but you came out after her.

BEA. I was livid.

ASH. I watched you grab her by her whole face.

BEA. She gave as good as she got.

ASH. She never let Dad drive that car – but on the way home she was crying so hard that Dad – he made her pull into a lay-by – and Mum got out of the car – and Dad got in her seat – and – and…
I thought that must've been the worst it got.

BEA. But it wasn't.

ASH. You can't fight with her today.

BEA. I'm not trying to.

ASH. I had this – this thought – I imagined – reading the eulogy – which is shit by the way – and I couldn't do it – and Dad couldn't do it – or didn't do anything – but you came up and you stood there – next to me – and you read – and I didn't have to – because you could – but that's not – you can't – can you? – and I had to see it – see you – see why – fucking shitpit – it's a fucking shitpit – and – and – and – and – I had to – I have to do it all – I have to / I have to –

BEA. / Ash.

ASH. And you're here –

BEA. Ash.

ASH. On the one day –

On the one / day –

BEA. / Ash.

ASH. You're here – and she'd never and / I can't –

BEA. / Please.

ASH. She'd never–
Mum'd never –

BEA. Please stop.

ASH. Do this to you.

BEA. I know.　　　　　　　　　ASH. She'd never do this
　　know.　　　　　　　　　　　　to you.
　　I know.　　　　　　　　　　　You know she wouldn't.
　　I know.　　　　　　　　　　　You know.
　　I know.
　　I know.
　　Breathe.
　　I know.　　　　　　　　　　ASH *can't catch his*
　　Breathe.　　　　　　　　　　*breath.*
　　I know.
　　In.
　　Breathe in.
　　Through your nose.
　　And out.
　　Mouth.
　　Breathe out through your mouth.

ASH. She knew – she knew – she knew it was going to – she knew it was going to be shit – she let it be shit – she / let –

BEA. / In, nose.
　　Out, / mouth.

ASH. / It's in a shithole because she didn't say –
　　She / didn't –

BEA. / Ash.

ASH. She didn't plan –
　　She didn't –

　　BEA *rubs circles on* ASH*'s back.*

BEA. It's okay.
　　You're okay.　　　　　　　ASH. No music.
　　You're okay.
　　Is that okay?
　　Can I do that?　　　　　　ASH *nods.*
　　Okay.
　　Lean back into me.

ASH *leans into* BEA.

Breathing in.
And hold.
And out.
And hold.
In.
Hold.
Out.
Hold.
You're like a bloody giraffe sit down.
In.
And out.

ASH*'s legs give way.*

He sits on the floor with BEA *behind him.*

That's it.
There we go.
That's it.

ASH *breathes*.

That's it.
You've got it.
You've got it.

BEA. Got your breath back?

ASH *half-nods, half-shakes his head*.

When you got stuck in the loos at the garden centre, I had to write the alphabet out on your back about a hundred times just to get you to calm down.

ASH *prickles*.

ASH. I don't remember.

BEA. You were so little.

BEA. Somewhere between two and three – you were a tiny little thing – a little acorn.

ASH. You could make up any old shit.

BEA. I know how they feel.

ASH. She didn't plan one thing.
No music.
Not a song.

BEA. No music at all?

ASH. Dad asked the person what the most popular songs were and picked the first one on the list and it's fucking 'Let it Be'.

BEA. No she'd hate that.

ASH. She'd HATE it.

BEA. Always very anti The Beatles.

ASH. And the few fucking people that'll be there are now always going to remember her with the fucking Beatles playing in the background and that's just wrong.

BEA. She liked 'Twist and Shout'.

ASH. What?

BEA *(singing)*. 'Twist and shout, twist and shout,
Come one, come on, come on now, baby, now'…

ASH. It's not good enough.

BEA. No.
No, it's not.
But you can't fit more than 'good enough' into thirty minutes…

ASH. That all it is?

BEA. Usually.

ASH. Thirty minutes?

BEA. Yes.

ASH. That's nothing.

BEA. No.

ASH. You wouldn't come for thirty minutes?

...

You said you loved me.

...

At the hospital you said you loved me.

...

BEA. Yeah.

ASH. I met this girl and she's – she's in Orlando – but she's – and she is a girl she's not a paedo like Mum thinks – but she ended things with me last night – she said she's not – she's not got the bandwidth – she's not emotionally available for – and I don't really understand that because we said we loved each other – but that it was all a bit too intense for her – and it fucks me off right because I was fine – I was – and she was the person I spoke to all the time – and I'd been saving all my birthday and Christmas money to visit her maybe after A levels but that's like – it's gone – it's gone because of something that didn't even happen to her – it didn't really happen to me – and I don't know what I've done – I don't know what I've done for people to be so fucking disappointing.

BEA. I do love you.

ASH. I want to know that she loved me.

BEA. This girl?

ASH. Mum.

BEA. She did.

ASH. But she didn't say it easily – she didn't really say it – and how embarrassing would it be to stand up in front of a room half-full of people loving Mum if she... didn't back.

BEA *fills with an incomprehensible volume of love for* ASH.

I've been trying really hard to remember the last time she

said she loved me and I think I've started just making stuff up in my head.

BEA. She wasn't a 'say it' kind of person.

ASH. Why not?

BEA. It's a very complicated thing.

ASH. It's not.
Even Dad said it – says it – more than her.
'Love you, mate'.
'Lots of love, mate'.
And he doesn't even like saying anything at all most of the time I don't think.

…

When she stopped getting her roots done I knew – I knew it was a dying-kind-of-ill – but she didn't tell me that – so I waited for…

BEA. I think she thought she had more time.

ASH. I told her I'd look after her.
And I would've looked after her.

BEA. I believe you.

ASH. She didn't.

BEA. Oh she believed you, that's why she wouldn't let you.

ASH. Makes no fucking sense.

BEA. I know.

ASH. I could've done it.

BEA. But she didn't want you to.

ASH. I don't get it.

BEA. She saw what it did to me.

ASH. What?

BEA. You're a child.

ASH. No I'm not.

BEA. She couldn't need her child like your grandpa needed me – it's a ruining, wild kind of need that sinks its teeth into the very best bits of a person.

ASH *sees* BEA *as a real person for the first time.*

She wouldn't have let herself need you like that.

ASH. The night she told me I made fajitas.
Old El Paso.
Bit of treat.
But she went round Diane's over the road and got twatted.

BEA. You did a nice thing.

ASH. But she didn't want it.

BEA. She wanted it too much maybe.

ASH. Nah.

BEA. Sometimes when I really want something, maybe something to eat, like I'm out at a restaurant, which is rare but, I might really want something, but I'll choose something else, because – I don't know why – it's like it's to spite myself – and I think your mum – I think we shared that.

ASH. But you can't do that to people.

BEA. Oh you can.

...

I used to think she wasn't nice enough to be a mum. It's horrible. I know it is. And you'd come here – before it was – so much like this – and you'd climb everything, play with everything, make forts, but once you crawled into a little nook and went so quiet. And your mum called your name. But you didn't answer. And she... lost it. She lost it like I didn't know anyone could lose it and she tore away at piles and piles of... my stuff. And she was screaming for you and screaming at me. And I was screaming at her because she was – she was – well, I didn't like the way she was moving everything. And I knew, then, she'd have gathered the strength to pick up this whole house if she had to just to find you safe. It was... the way she held you when she found you – you'd fallen asleep – if you'd seen it, you'd know.

ASH. But I didn't.

BEA. Then I'll tell you about it.

ASH. It's... hard... because... I feel so... angry like so... because you and her weren't... because if you were close... I could believe you... because she would've told you about me... so I could believe – she didn't leave a letter or anything.

BEA. That kind of only happens in films.

ASH. I know what it'd say.
Write neater so examiners can mark your work.
Go to a Russell Group university.
Those games are rotting your brain.
Don't wear joggers outside the house – but also just leave the fucking house more.

BEA *laughs*.

That was the content of most of her speeches after half a bottle of rosé on a Friday night.

...

Before you woke up, at the hospital, it felt a bit like being with Mum.

BEA. What happened then – I'm – I'm very very embarrassed.

ASH. You told me I was lying.

BEA. I'm so sorry.

ASH. I wanted to be lying.

BEA. The world felt really wobbly.

ASH. You said she'd been here.

BEA *flounders*.

She hated it here.

BEA. I know.

ASH. You were so sure.

BEA. And now I'm not.

ASH. It is a bonsai.

> BEA *is thrown*.

I do have a bonsai.

> BEA *smiles*.

It's called Herb.

BEA. What kind?

ASH. Juniper.

> *Something changes in the air between* ASH *and* BEA.

You had one.

BEA. Mine's a Chinese Elm.

ASH. Why did you say it?

BEA. I don't know.

ASH. How did you know?

> BEA *can't answer*.

Things like… that… things like what you said don't happen in real life.

BEA. Then it didn't happen in real life.

ASH. There was a guy – a park ranger – in Virginia – got struck by lightning seven times.

BEA. That's… unlucky.

ASH. Unlucky to be struck, lucky to survive each time.

BEA. Don't know what's worse.

ASH. Said he saw the afterlife – each time – people he'd known.

BEA. Yeah?

ASH. Yeah.

BEA. Did he say what it was like?

ASH. Rest of the article was behind a paywall.

BEA. He still alive?

ASH. Don't know, killed himself, I think.

BEA. Oh.

...

ASH. Why are you like this?

BEA. It's a horrible mulch of things in me.

ASH. But you had people.

BEA. What do you mean?

ASH. You had my mum.
And your dad.

BEA. People get tired of what a stubborn thing it is.

ASH. Because they let it go on.

BEA. Because it hurts too much.

ASH. And this doesn't?

BEA. I've chosen this house and these things over every person that has ever tried to help.

...

After our mum – because of how in-an-instant it was – we just coped however we could – we coped in different – scratch that – no – we didn't cope – we didn't cope – we held on – just about – for as long as we could – but – and I'm not sure who really let go first – but the more I lost – and had to lose – the worse it got.

ASH. I want her.

BEA. I know.

ASH. I keep thinking she's gonna walk through the door.

BEA. Hang on a second.

>BEA *disappears.*
>
>*As he waits,* ASH *looks around the room.*
>
>*His curiosity grows.*
>
>*He pokes around.*
>
>*Suddenly, there is an avalanche of cutlery.*

ASH. FUCK

>BEA *reappears with a cloth bag.*

BEA. Are you alright?

ASH. You've got a lot of cutlery.

BEA. Yeah.

ASH. A lot.

BEA. Yeah. I've got a lot of cutlery. I've got fucking mountains of it. More than the average IKEA.

ASH. Why?

BEA. Because it makes me feel safe.

ASH. Really?

BEA. Unbelievably.

ASH. Safe?

BEA. Do you remember the little green men who sailed away on a sieve?

ASH. No.

BEA. You liked it.

ASH. Okay.

BEA. Me and your mum, our mum, she used to read it to us – I wouldn't get in the bath without my sieve.

ASH. Because sieves were boats.

BEA. And I wanted to make them sail.
And then forks became girls with plaits in their hair and knives became boys with bald heads.

ASH. What about spoons?

BEA. They were always old people for some reason.

ASH. So…?

BEA. For as long as I can remember, forks and knives and spoons weren't metal, they were people, people afraid to be picked and people afraid of not being picked.

ASH. What's worse?

BEA. Not getting picked. Made me worry they'd feel sad.

ASH. Are you still…?

BEA. Like this?

ASH. Yeah.

BEA. Oh yes.
…

One birthday, this was before my mum died, because it started before then, I can't remember which one, but I remember purple paper plates and plastic forks for cake – and I remember there being just one little fork left in the plastic pouch, one little extra that nobody needed, and I remember not knowing what else to do but kiss that little girl fork. Just to let her know she wasn't unwanted. Just to make her feel special. And I kept her on me all day. Until I sat down too quick, and she stabbed me in the belly. So later on I snuck off to my room and I put her in my bed, tucked her in, and told her I'd be back in a bit – and I've never told anyone that before.

ASH. I used to chew crisps until they were paste, spit them out, roll them into a ball, put them on the radiator for a bit to warm up, and then eat them again.

BEA. Did you really?

ASH. Yeah.

BEA. That's brilliant.
And disgusting.

> BEA *holds out the bag to* ASH.
>
> ASH *looks in the bag.*

ASH. Keys?

BEA. I glued most of them back together but the rest of it's in about a hundred pieces.

ASH. You play?

BEA. No, that was her thing.

ASH. My hands aren't very good at working together.

BEA. Neither are mine.

ASH. Really annoyed her.

BEA. Her piano teacher would swipe her hands right off the keys if she ever made a mistake.

ASH. Really?

BEA. Really.

ASH. I'd still take piano with Mum over times-tables with Dad.

BEA. That bad?

> ASH *empties the bag of keys out onto the carpet.*
>
> *He starts separating them into piles of black keys and white keys.*

ASH. Easier to start with the black keys.

BEA. Is it?

ASH (*placing them as he counts*). They go two… then three… two… three… two… three… two… you can help…

> BEA *kneels down next to* ASH.

Three… two… and three… and then the white.

BEA. There's still a bit missing off this one.

ASH. Couldn't find it?

BEA. Needle in a haystack.

ASH. Just put it at the end.

> BEA *arranges some white keys.*

No that's too many white ones there.

BEA. How many do you want?

ASH. Two white keys in the gap between the set of two black and the set of three black – and then one between each black key.

Together, they arrange the keys.

Last one goes here.

BEA. Done.

> ASH *and* BEA *look at their creation.*

Feels like we've just invented the piano.

ASH. But it doesn't work.

BEA. Doesn't it?

ASH. No.

BEA. You haven't even tried it.

ASH. Don't do that.

BEA. What?

ASH. Just don't.

> BEA *wills* ASH – *almost cosmically.*
>
> ASH *reaches out to touch a key.*

No.

BEA. Ash.

ASH. This is –

It's just pieces.
You can't play.
They're not really real.
They're not what they should be.
They're not where they should be.
They're just –

BEA *plays a note – the note sounds.*

ASH *doesn't know what he heard.*

BEA. I know I can't hold on to it any more.

ASH *is still.*

I finished glueing the last key this morning.
It was the only thing that felt right.

ASH *hovers a finger over a key.*

ASH. Start by finding Middle C.

He plays a note.

The note sounds.

BEA. What were you going to say today?

ASH *shrugs.*

Don't shrug it's rude.

ASH. Sorry.

BEA. Just let this house hear it.

ASH *pulls out his phone.*

ASH. It's not even really in full sentences.

BEA. Doesn't matter.

ASH. I'm not good at stuff like this.

BEA. Who is?

ASH *looks at his phone notes.*

ASH. It's like the weakest starting sentence ever.

BEA. What is it?

ASH. It's embarrassing.

BEA. Go on.

ASH. This whole thing is embarrassing.

BEA. It's only me.

> ASH *relents.*
>
> *He prepares.*

ASH. My mum was a great mum. She loved reading and *Dancing on Ice* and rosé and eating outside in the garden. She was –
See it's fucking stupid.

BEA. I mean, you've got her.

ASH. I want to say that Mum managed the shit out of everything.

BEA. Yeah?

ASH. Yeah, everything happened because Mum happened.

BEA. What else?

ASH. Mum happened so we happened.
Me.
And Dad.
And I don't know how we do it now.
I don't know how to make things happen now.
Because Mum always gave me timings.
'You've got half an hour before the bus.'
'Dinner is ready in five.'
'If you're not in the car in ten we're going without you!'
But I don't feel like anything's going to happen any more.
I don't feel a rush.
I'm not where I should be.

BEA. It'll come back – time – it does.

ASH. I'm not where I should be.

BEA. When your grandpa died I didn't eat for days, I forgot, completely forgot until days later about two in the morning when I got up, walked to the petrol garage in my pyjamas

and bought a sausage roll. I'm a vegetarian. But it shocked
my body back into existing.
Because you-things will happen again.
There will be a moment when you realise that you're still
alive.
And I don't mean in a philosophical way.
And not in a stoic way, either.
Fuck the stoics.
They're always men with wives who do everything for them.
No.
Just in a bodily way.
Because you have needs.
Needs that are the difference between life and death.
It's hunger.
That's what pierces first.

ASH. Will you be there?

BEA. I will.

ASH. Okay.

BEA. Now this is your two-minute warning because we
are getting the fuck out here and we are going to that
crematorium, and it doesn't matter if it's over or if it's a
shithole because we are going to go and we are going to do
what we can and we are going to say goodbye.

ASH. How?

BEA. I'm going to call a friend – a colleague – a friend who
I know with a car because we have to go.

ASH. We have to go.

BEA. We have to go.

ASH. We have to fucking go.

BEA. No choice.

ASH. Now.

BEA hugs ASH.

BEA. Sorry sorry no time sorry.

BEA *grabs whatever's closest to her – her bag, her keys, her raincoat.*

As she does, she reveals VEDA*'s coat.*

ASH *notices the coat.*

Come on.

ASH *doesn't move.*

What is it?

ASH *is stunned.*

ASH. That's Mum's.

BEA *knows now.*

BEA. Always got her hand-me-downs.

ASH. She loves that coat.

BEA. Come on, let's go.
Come on, after you.

ASH *exits.*

BEA *goes over to* VEDA*'s coat.*

She looks at the label.

Pure alpaca my arse, you're eighty per cent polyester.

BEA *gives the coat a big squeeze.*

End.